OUR BILL OF RIGHTS

A JURY OF YOUR PEERS

A LOOK AT THE SIXTH AND SEVENTH AMENDMENTS

RACHAEL MORLOCK

PowerKiDS press.

NEW YORK

Published in 2019 by The Rosen Publishing Group, Inc.
29 East 21st Street, New York, NY 10010

Editor: Sharon Gleason
Book Design: Rachel Rising

Photo Credits: Cover Fuse/Corbis/Getty Images; Cover, pp. 1, 3, 4, 5, 6, 7, 8, 9, 10, 11, 12, 14, 15, 16, 17, 18, 20, 22, 23, 24, 25, 26, 27, 28, 29, 30, 31, 32 (background) Mad Dog/Shutterstock.com; Cover, pp. 1, 3, 4, 5, 6, 7, 8, 9, 10, 11, 12, 14, 15, 16, 17, 18, 20, 22, 23, 24, 25, 26, 27, 28, 29, 30, 31, 32 (background) Flas100/Shutterstock.com; pp. 5, 9, 13, 23 Bettman/Contributor/Getty Images; pp. 6, 8, 10, 24, 28 (arrows) Forest Foxy/Shutterstock.com; p. 7 David Frazier/The Image Bank/Getty Images; p. 11 Universal History Archive/ Universal Image Group/Getty Images; p. 13 (insert) Courtesy of the Library of Congress; p. 15 Everett Historical/Shutterstock.com; p. 16 wavebreakmedia/ Shutterstock.com; p. 17 Print Collector/Hulton Fine Art Collection/Getty Images; p. 19 https://commons.wikimedia.org/ wiki/File:Nixon_edited_transcripts.jpg; p. 21 New York Daily News Archive/New York Daily News/Getty Images; p. 25 Joseph Sohm/Shutterstock.com; pp. 26, 29 sirtravelalot/Shutterstock.com; p. 27 Culture Club/Hulton Archive/Getty Images.

Cataloging-in-Publication Data

Names: Morlock, Rachael.
Title: A jury of your peers: a look at the sixth and seventh amendments / Rachael Morlock.
Description: New York : PowerKids Press, 2019. | Series: Our Bill of Rights | Includes glossary and index.
Identifiers: ISBN 9781538343043 (pbk.) | ISBN 9781538343067 (library bound) | ISBN 9781538343050 (6 pack)
Subjects: LCSH: Due process of law--United States--Juvenile literature. | Jury--United States--Juvenile literature. | United States. Constitution. 6th Amendment--Juvenile literature. | United States. Constitution. 5th Amendment--Juvenile literature.
Classification: LCC KF4765.M68 2019 | DDC 345.73'056--dc23

Manufactured in the United States of America

CPSIA Compliance Information: Batch #CWPK19 For further information contact Rosen Publishing, New York, New York at 1-800-237-9932.

CONTENTS

THE BILL OF RIGHTS

After long months of discussions and arguments, the Founding Fathers signed the U.S. Constitution on September 17, 1787. The Articles of Confederation had failed to unite America. With the Constitution, greater powers were given to the government in order to strengthen the nation.

Next, the states considered the Constitution for acceptance. As they did, many created lists of rights that they felt needed protection from the federal government. James Madison combined these suggestions into a list of proposed amendments, or changes, to the Constitution. Ten of his suggested changes were approved by the states and became known as the Bill of Rights.

KNOW YOUR RIGHTS!

The right to trial by jury is described both in the Bill of Rights and in the third article of the Constitution.

In 1776, George Mason wrote the Virginia Declaration of Rights. Many of Mason's words and ideas were later included in the Bill of Rights, including the promise of trial by jury.

Two of the 10 amendments in the Bill of Rights deal with the right to trial by jury. American colonists viewed trial by jury as a powerful tool for **democracy** and justice. The Sixth and Seventh Amendments secure this right for Americans in criminal and civil cases.

TRIAL BY JURY

In England, trial by jury has been central to courts for hundreds of years. The practice was featured in the Magna Carta of 1215, which outlined English laws. The English Bill of Rights of 1689 also stated the importance of an impartial, or fair, jury and banned excessive fines or bail, which is money paid to free prisoners until their trial.

In England and America, juries were seen as the best way to promise a fair trial and control corrupt, or dishonest, powers in court. However, in the Declaration of Independence, Americans accused the British of **"depriving** us in many cases, of the benefits of Trial by Jury." Later, the leaders of the American government secured those benefits with the Sixth and Seventh Amendments.

Trial by jury includes the jury and a judge who oversees the trial. This is different from a bench trial, which is a trial in which the decision is made by at least one judge.

JUDGES AND JURIES

In a jury trial, a group of citizens listens to the facts of a case and delivers its decision, also known as a verdict. Since the jury is made up of ordinary citizens, the judge is there to share expert knowledge of the law and keep the trial moving smoothly. The judge can also give the jurors important instructions or explanations that will help them make a fair decision.

CRIMINAL TRIALS

Every amendment in the Bill of Rights checks the power of the government. After suffering from unjust British practices, the creators of the Constitution and the Bill of Rights wanted to prevent their government from unfairly trying citizens accused of crimes. Trial by jury limits the role of government by giving ordinary citizens the power to deliver justice.

The Sixth Amendment protects the right to a jury trial in criminal cases. In a criminal case, a **defendant** is accused of breaking the law by the government, represented by a **prosecutor**. The Sixth Amendment also lists the defendant's rights in court. The trial must be speedy, public, and impartial. Defendants deserve to know the charges and witnesses they face and to have legal help. Each right helps build the framework for a fair and lawful trial.

Rosa Parks and others participated in a bus **boycott** in Montgomery, Alabama, in 1956. When Parks went to trial for breaking an antiboycott law, the Sixth Amendment protected her rights as a defendant.

THE SIXTH AMENDMENT

"In all criminal prosecutions, the accused shall enjoy the right to a speedy and public trial, by an impartial jury of the State and district wherein the crime shall have been committed, which district shall have been previously ascertained by law, and to be informed of the nature and cause of the accusation; to be confronted with the witnesses against him; to have compulsory process for obtaining witnesses in his favor, and to have the Assistance of Counsel for his defense."

SPEEDY TRIALS

In the words of the Sixth Amendment, "the accused shall enjoy the right to a speedy and public trial." The Speedy Trial Act of 1974 establishes time limits for bringing a defendant to trial. If the trial isn't held in a speedy manner, the trial and charges must be dropped.

Before American independence, colonists were sometimes transported to England to face charges. These defendants endured extremely long delays and separation from their work, home, and families. The Constitution's framers responded to these unfavorable colonial experiences. They required a speedy trial in the "state and district" where the crime was committed. However, it is lawful to move a trial to another location in cases where local publicity may affect the jury's verdict.

In 1872, Susan B. Anthony was arrested at her Rochester, New York, home for voting illegally. Anthony's story became a popular local topic. Her trial was moved out of Rochester to avoid a **biased** jury.

REASONS FOR SPEED

Delays before a trial sometimes can have harmful effects. Evidence for the trial can be lost or destroyed, and witnesses' memories can fade or change. In addition, a long delay before a trial might harm the defendant's reputation and health. Speedy trials are more likely to be fair. Although prosecutors can't cause lengthy delays, defendants can request extra time in order to prepare their defense.

PUBLIC TRIALS

A trial is public if members of the community and media can attend. By requiring public trials, the Sixth Amendment exposes the operation of the justice system to the American people. It compels court officials and witnesses to be honest, responsible, and subject to outside judgment. In 1914, shortly before Louis Brandeis became a Supreme Court justice, he said, "Sunshine is said to be the best of disinfectants," meaning if the court operates in full view of the public, then it's more likely to act justly.

Of course, there are several important exceptions. If safety or public security are at stake, then all or part of a trial can be closed to the public. Sometimes, the **testimony** of child witnesses and victims may occur in private to avoid pain and embarrassment.

KNOW YOUR RIGHTS!

In 17th-century England under Charles I, many individuals were tried in secret by the Star Chamber. This often unjust, closed court served as a warning against private trials.

In 1925, John T. Scopes was tried for illegal teachings. Large audiences attended the popular trial, which was the first trial broadcast live on the radio.

JOHN T. SCOPES

13

AN IMPARTIAL JURY

The Sixth Amendment promises the right to a jury of peers. A number of rules prevent bias in the jury. First, a jury pool is created from individuals who live in the area where the crime occurred. The jury pool should represent the people in the community in terms of race, **ethnicity**, and gender (male or female). Next, the lawyers on both sides of the case have an opportunity to ask questions. Each side can select or ban individuals in the pool as they choose jurors.

The jury's job is to find out the facts of a case. The jurors study evidence and listen to witnesses. When it's time to decide a case, their verdict must be unanimous, meaning that all the jurors agree.

KNOW YOUR RIGHTS!

Juries have the power to acquit, which means if there is reasonable doubt that the defendant committed the crime, a jury can decide the defendant is not guilty.

CIVIC DUTY

Serving on a jury is an important **civic** duty. It's an opportunity for citizens to take an active part in their government and the justice system. The Founding Fathers believed that the common sense of ordinary people should play a powerful role in the government. Jurors make decisions that affect many people's lives. They must be fair, honest, and committed to finding the truth.

U.S. juries originally only included white men. Since those days, Supreme Court decisions made it illegal to keep someone from being a juror based on gender, race, or ethnicity. Juries should be diverse, or varied, since society is diverse.

THE RIGHT TO BE INFORMED

Defendants have the right to know the charges against them. The Sixth Amendment requires that the person being accused of a crime "be informed of the nature and cause of the accusation." The charges must be specific, include the date and time of the crime, and note the laws that were broken. If they're informed, then defendants are better able to prepare a defense.

The 1637 trial of John Lilburne in England influenced American lawmakers. Since he wasn't told the charges against him, Lilburne refused to participate in his trial. He was punished and sent to prison.

In addition to knowing the charges, defendants also have the right to know who accuses them. The confrontation clause of the Sixth Amendment requires that a defendant is "confronted with the witnesses against him." This is another piece of valuable information that can help defendants prepare for the arguments and evidence they'll use in court.

CONFRONTATION AND COMPULSORY PROCESS

The confrontation clause allows defendants to know who accuses them. Defendants can be present in the courtroom and challenge witnesses as they testify. Witnesses may be cross-examined, or questioned by the other side, in court. When they testify face to face, witnesses are more likely to tell the truth. In some rare cases, witnesses and experts can provide long-distance or out-of-court testimony. Usually, witnesses must be available for cross-examination.

In addition to confronting witnesses for the prosecution, defendants also have the right to obtain their own witnesses. Compulsory process helps the defense secure witnesses with information that can help their case. Courts can order people to testify or produce evidence. In addition, defendants have the right to testify on their own behalf, which means they are allowed to defend themselves.

KNOW YOUR RIGHTS!

A subpoena is an official order to provide evidence or serve as a witness in a trial or investigation. It's against the law to disobey a subpoena.

President Richard Nixon refused a subpoena to provide tape recordings during the Watergate investigation in the 1970s. The case of *United States v. Nixon* in 1974 decided that even the president must obey subpoenas.

THE RIGHT TO COUNSEL

Since the Bill of Rights was written, the legal system has become increasingly difficult to understand. Defendants have little chance of proving their innocence without the help of knowledgeable lawyers. The Sixth Amendment promises "the Assistance of Counsel." Several Supreme Court decisions have developed the right to have a legal representative and advisor in court.

In *Gideon v. Wainwright* (1963), the Supreme Court recognized that not all defendants are able to pay for a lawyer. When defendants face jail time, the government must provide them with a lawyer. This applies to federal and state trials. However, having a lawyer isn't enough. The case of *Strickland v. Washington* (1984) requires court-appointed counsel to be effective in securing a fair trial for defendants.

KNOW YOUR RIGHTS!

Court-appointed lawyers who are paid by the government are called public defenders. Many public defenders often have to serve more than one defendant during the same time period.

The "Scottsboro Boys" trial in 1931 showed the importance of effective counsel. Court-appointed lawyers for nine young men were unqualified and unprepared. A later Supreme Court decision reversed the trial's severe sentences.

CIVIL TRIALS

While the Sixth Amendment concerns criminal trials, the Seventh Amendment refers to civil trials. Civil trials involve losses or **damages** instead of crimes. They take place when a **plaintiff** sues a defendant either for money or to put a stop to actions that are causing harm. Civil cases can include lawsuits relating to car accidents, employment, contracts, **copyright** issues, and civil rights.

The Seventh Amendment includes two main parts. First, the preservation clause outlines the civil cases that can be tried by a jury. Other civil suits will be heard by a judge. Next, the reexamination clause declares that the decision of a civil case tried by a jury is final in most cases. This protects the decisions of a jury from the power of a federal judge.

KNOW YOUR RIGHTS!

Although civil juries are an English tradition, today the United States is one of the only nations to require civil jury trials.

THE SEVENTH AMENDMENT

"In Suits at common law, where the value in **controversy** shall exceed twenty dollars, the right of trial by jury shall be preserved, and no fact tried by a jury, shall be otherwise re-examined in any Court of the United States, than according to the rules of the common law."

In the civil trial of *Grimshaw v. Ford Motor Company* (1978), Ford was found guilty of producing a car called a Pinto that easily started on fire. The jury fined Ford millions of dollars in damages.

RESISTING TYRANNY

In the years before the American Revolutionary War, British laws and taxes dramatically affected American lives. By serving on civil juries, colonists had an opportunity to resist the unpopular laws because they could rule in favor of Americans.

After the Revolution, the right to civil jury trials was notably absent from the Constitution. Federalists, who supported a strong central government, felt that civil juries would threaten justice. They believed that since Americans would elect their lawmakers, there was no reason to check the government's power through civil juries. Anti-Federalists believed protection against corrupt government and bad laws were still necessary. In the end, civil juries were included in the Bill of Rights.

This colonial courtroom is preserved in Colonial Williamsburg, Virginia. Many states, including Virginia, suggested including civil juries in the Constitution.

BEFORE THE BILL OF RIGHTS

The Seventh Amendment had important **precedents**. Several states had already included such protections in their constitutions. George Mason wrote an early form of the Seventh Amendment within the Virginia Declaration of Rights in 1776. It said, "That in controversies respecting property, and in suits between man and man, the ancient trial by jury is preferable to any other and ought to be held sacred."

COMMON LAW

The Seventh Amendment allows "suits at common law" for jury trials. In 18th-century England, cases were divided into specific groups. Some cases were always decided by a judge. Common law cases were decided by juries. The amendment supports these distinctions—the kind of cases that would have been tried by English juries should be tried by American juries.

In the common law case of *Wilkes v. Wood* (1763), an English jury awarded John Wilkes damages for the illegal search of his home. This influenced the American commitment to civil jury trials.

The Supreme Court case of *Dimick v. Schiedt* (1935) declared that the Seventh Amendment refers specifically to the common law of England in 1791, when the Bill of Rights was ratified, or approved. The rules of common law at that time should be used to determine which civil cases can be tried by juries.

THE SUBSTANCE OF THE SEVENTH

In modern American life, there are many legal situations that would've been unimaginable to English courts in 1791. The Supreme Court has responded to this challenge as new types of civil trials become common. In these cases, the meaning of the Seventh Amendment must be carefully considered.

In the case of *Baltimore & Carolina Line, Inc. v. Redman* (1935), the Supreme Court ruled that, "The aim of the Amendment is to preserve the substance of the common law right of trial by jury, as **distinguished** from mere matters of form or procedure." This decision opens more civil cases up to the possibility of trial by jury. However, it also loosens the rules for civil jury trials. As a result, the functions and structure of civil juries have changed.

Historically, juries were made up of 12 individuals. In the case of *Colgrove v. Battin* (1973), the Supreme Court decided that civil juries can be composed of only six jurors.

FEDERAL AND STATE

Originally, the Bill of Rights protected citizens' freedom from the federal government. The Constitution's framers thought it was important to keep federal and state governments separate. More recently, the Supreme Court has extended much of the Bill of Rights to the states. Most of the Sixth Amendment must be followed in state trials as well as federal trials. However, state trials are not required to follow the Seventh Amendment.

JURY TRIALS TODAY

America's founders believed the right to trial by jury was important in creating a free and just government. Juries played a central role in allowing colonial Americans to respond to unfair laws. They gave Americans the opportunity to be active in government and stand up to corrupt powers.

Today, jury trials are rare. Trial by jury can be a long and expensive process. In criminal trials, plea bargains rule out trial by jury. Many civil lawsuits are decided out of court or by judges, and less than 1 percent are decided by juries. Despite these trends, the Sixth and Seventh Amendments still protect the rights of Americans on trial. They reflect the fundamental belief that ordinary citizens have an important role to play in their government.

KNOW YOUR RIGHTS!

Plea bargains, in which the defendant pleads guilty to a less serious charge, are used in about 97 percent of criminal cases. In a plea bargain, defendants give up their right to trial by jury.

GLOSSARY

bias: An unfair preference for or dislike of something or someone.

boycott: To join with others in refusing to buy from or deal with a person, nation, or business.

civic: Relating to a citizen, a city, or citizenship.

controversy: An argument in which people express strong opposing views.

copyright: The legal right to be the only one to reproduce, publish, or sell the contents and form of a literary, musical, or artistic work.

damage: Harm caused, or a sum of money given to make up for that harm.

defendant: A person who is being sued or accused of a crime in a court of law.

democracy: A government elected by the people, either directly or indirectly.

deprive: To take something away from someone or something.

distinguish: To know or point out a difference.

ethnicity: The state of belonging to a group of people with a certain origin or background.

plaintiff: The complaining party in a lawsuit.

precedent: Something that may serve as an example or rule to be followed in the future.

prosecutor: The lawyer in a criminal case trying to prove that the accused person is guilty.

testimony: A statement made by a witness in court.

INDEX

WEBSITES

Due to the changing nature of Internet links, PowerKids Press has developed an online list of
websites related to the subject of this book. This site is updated regularly. Please use this link to
access the list: www.powerkidslinks.com/obor/sixthseventh